Last City

Last City

Brian Sneeden

Carnegie Mellon University Press
Pittsburgh 2018

Acknowledgments

Grateful acknowledgment is made to the following publications in which some of these poems first appeared:

Arion: "Persephone," "Phthisis: A Letter"
Asheville Poetry Review: "The Temple"
Beloit Poetry Journal: "The Road"
Boulevard: "Bryshen and the Burning House"
Denver Quarterly: "Study for Two Figures"
Harvard Review Online: "Flamenco"
The Hollins Critic: "The Hermit, Having a Lantern"
The Journal: "Gion"
The Literary Review: "Dogmoon," "Goodbye-harvest"
The Malahat Review: "The Island"
Mid-American Review: "Alexandria Duet"
Ninth Letter: "Lord's Prayer," "Mist Burial"
Prairie Schooner: "Elegy in Which I Am Awake"
Quarterly West: "The River of the Given"
Salt Hill: "Squatters"
Southern Humanities Review: "The Crystal Cave," "Stratis the Sailor at Eleusis"
Southern Poetry Review: "Ode to Future Thirst"
storySouth: "Again Is the First Time"
Third Coast: "Ghosts"
TriQuarterly: "After a Suicide"
Virginia Quarterly Review: "Last City," "Reconstruction"

"Flamenco" and "Persephone" appeared in Greek translation in Τεφλόν (*Teflon*); "Flamenco" and "The Crystal Cave" appeared in Serbian translation in *Eckermann*.

Cover art: *Diamond*, by David Fleck, 297 x 420mm, pen and ink, 2012, 2017

Carnegie Mellon University Press wishes to acknowledge—with great appreciation— the generous support of Courtney and Lisa Cox.

Book design by Danielle Lehmann

Library of Congress Control Number 2017950746
ISBN 978-0-88748-634-0
Copyright © 2018 by Brian Sneeden
Printed and bound in the United States of America

10 9 8 7 6 5 4 3 2 1

for Arabella

Contents

III.

There is no new land, no new sea:
the city will follow you.

—C. P. Cavafy

Last City

Perhaps it is the matter of going out
which bothers me. That you or I

or someone we know will have to get up,
wearing only the warmth of the memory

of our clothes, and find an airy socket
in the car-fumed street. They say

it is possible, for those who go quickly
or who are born with only one soul

to slip out with dignity, from the back row
at an opera, and into a black cab

with plush seats and tinted windows full
of aquarium lights. But what about

the rest—the underdressed millions
forced to rise and leave with the curtain

still up, and the sound of someone's voice
lingering on the air. Do they file

one by one into the street, leaving behind
a pair of gloves or a half-touched

glass of wine, waiting for no one to arrive
and offer to pay the fare? But then

who's to say that you and I, busy making
small talk with someone or another

on the last sidewalk, couldn't manage
to find a road of our own, and a ride.

I

Squatters

By doing nothing

they are building a room for the rain.
In April sparrows fly in. October,
and they rake the leaves into a wall

to give the silence something to do.
Sometimes one of them will hear
music coming from behind the door

but when he looks to see, it is only
the cold night sky. When they sleep
noises come out, like hands unfolding

from the stone: a slur of bare feet,
or the clink like a thrush prodding
an invisible hole. After ten years

it is theirs—all of it. The gardens
and the sinks. The broken window
in the small ruined wall looking out

on another window. The dead lovers
Maro and Renald, still loitering on
the stairs, hoisting the same transparent

jug of wine. All of it, but the room
for the rain, with the roof half-eaten
by the bright mineral light of the moon.

Bryshen and the Burning House

I do not hear your music anymore
only its shadow, which is the same
as a memory without blood. Like when
a house is on fire, and some flame
sneaks into the instrument cases,
finding them used and, I think,
nutritious for a flame, and eats both
the last song and the first, and also
your ten thousand fingerprints. Who
will enter the house now, picking
from the ash a single peg like a burning
tooth? But at least there's these letters.
Tell me again how did it go, the one
that started with the Ukrainian night.

Goodbye-harvest

Often the girl sitting alone on the roof.
        Often the cat in heat.
Often the rim of the bucket
growing mold after a death
        in the house, waiting
to be taken out so death cannot wash
his sword in it.
Often he washes his feet
        on the roof, with his hair
falling out over the village in moonlight.
Do you remember the moonlight.
Often the bird singing
with the string in its throat. Often
        the empty furnace, and the snow
which makes you younger.
Often the late shadow,
and the stain which circles in the wine
after a death in the house
like a ballet shoe crusted in rosin,
        waiting. Often
the woman sitting alone on the rock
wearing only the howl of a dog
washing her village in darkness,
her hair falling out across the water
at Amorgos
where shipwrecks grow like wheat.
        Often my goodbye-harvest
of twice-broken things
emptied in the sea. Do you remember
the sea, waiting to be taken out.

The River of the Given

Let it go, that which you gave to me.

Put it in the water and let it float

or sink as it can, without our help,

without our touching it each time

the old need arises, and the reaching

muscle starts again. Put it in

the water and see if it folds

to one side, or manages to pull along

straight and even on top of its own

reflection, with its bright string

attached to the edge of something

far out. Without nourishment,

without the miraculous human DNA

threading its tiniest bone to ours—

watch and see how far it goes

on the food of its own breath,

like a pharaoh bundle drifting

among the fingerbumps of the reeds.

Give it back to where you found it

beneath the foam and debris,

weighing less than its shadow

on the air, before you spoke it a body

and the rest: heat, noise, name—

times when you did not know

you touched, and an invisible blood

passed into the thought and grew heavy,

until it sprouted hair, teeth. Put it

in the water now and let it go

to where the river starts over,

to where the parts of us gradually

flake off, and it can be again

someone's food, someone's joy.

Reconstruction

*But, my dear sirs, when peace does come, you may call on me for
any thing. Then will I share with you the last cracker.*
—General Sherman, "Letter to Atlanta"

They put their guns in the only boxes
they had, and those the well-
liquored strips of gin barrels
wrapped in hemp, and buried them
in the troughs of their once-fields
of burnt clay. The black went down
six feet, so they said,
until one of the shovels struck
a hemp root, *the last root*
in Georgia, and threw them in
while reciting from a Bible
something around the Canaanites,
and thought about the barrels rusting
in their musty barrelwoods. Everyone
could play the fiddle, but those were gone
with the woodwinds—so they sat
one by one and talked about
the acrid earth in their mouths
like burnt bread as one hums
a negro song, and the others,
finding they can speak the words
begin to sing, loudly, howling,
until one says, *shit son,*
you'd think we're trying to call them back.

Mist Burial

I bury you in the heron's eye.

Who will tell me
        when the birds come again to Patmos,
singing the song of bitter lemons
over the water.
        Or when a fisherman
pulls up some statue from the harbor
caught in his net—
        Our Lady of the Vanishing Sorrow,
Lady of the Forgotten Name—
with half of her face eaten
        by drachma-fish
and moonlight. Who will say
at night, when the spark of a woman
        lighting a match in a doorway
opens for a moment
the sea,
        like a goatherd's lamp
in a field at dusk, drunk,
stumbling in alertness.
        At dawn the last boat
comes back
with urgent news for someone
        and the air changes
inside the porticos,
around the hands pressing open
        and closing the shutters—who will say
which silence
has taken root, and if it is the same one
        you told me
grows at the foot of the volcano

once a lifetime,
      and when it ripens
takes the voice of a young girl
and buries it
      half in the air and half in the sea.

Dogmoon

In the movie the dog on Earth lives
while the dog in space stays in space.
Waiting, barking. Licking in silence
the metal rivets of the astropod,
until her shadow becomes subtracted
from data's shadow. What
animates when the animating spirit
moves on? On Earth: a fabric of leaf
moved by accident
like dust moved on an adjusted picture frame,
nothing of consequence, a little wind,
the decay of laughter in a brightening hall.
But think of Laika, cowering in holes of air
beneath the great metal wings of a satellite.
Hearing no master, curling up
at no one's feet. Leaving again
her fern-like bones scattered, buried
beneath trees in space. Occasionally
one still falls and lights up
hyacinth in the air over Tokyo
uncounted, just another colored light.

Assets

They say the wind was sold
to a banker in New York for peanuts.
That he taught it to run alone

back and forth in an empty room
so that he could say, later, at dinner parties,
with his thumb inside a martini,

there was one thing in the world
that was only his. And that he came back
late one night to find it dead: exhaustion

from no purpose, and he thought
perhaps loneliness is worse
after it has been tried to be fixed.

Again Is the First Time

It is possible to have everything,
like listening for a music in the music.
Somehow I am walking down Patton
and Walnut, and somehow it is there—
the primordial quivering, catching a whiff
of magnitude down a side street:
a quality of sun and air, or the pairing
of two dead leaves on the sidewalk just so.
Turning, I pass a woman in a turtleneck,
a dog tied to a bench and find
the man who owes me twenty dollars.
It is possible to have everything, or at least
twenty dollars, which is also everything
when I spend it on a Death in the Afternoon
for my wife and myself, the champagne
and absinthe mixed to form a sort of cloud.
Like when I walked the Rue Delambre, at night,
blossoming inward like a chrysanthemum
for a small view of the Seine, and thought
for once, surely now is enough. To arrive
this late and still be the first. Like the body
saying, *again for the first time.* What
is everywhere offers itself, again, itself.

Ghosts

They have come in the night and cut down
all the Bradford pears. Now I walk
beneath nothing, the severed half-row
and their whiteness gone. The hum
of the chainsaw, lingering in the eaves and
doorways like the husk of absence—the place
of their bodies where I watched
in spring, a stranger then, your hand
pluck a white blossom, cupping it in the palm
like your very own corner in the spotless.
Now I enter it, fit my body to the wound
of them not there, thinking that I owed it
to myself for their sake, just this once
to be alive with what echoes: a foot,
a hum, a cat, a lamp, a key. The wound
that emptied you still emptying.

Study for Two Figures

Like the human shadow, if you were to remove
    a single ingredient—say, the soul—
all would collapse, like a building made of rain
    and probably with the sound of a dozen
unseen people clearing their throats. You were so
    tiny then, like a painting on the air,
torn apart by a thought or the slightest dark
    of water, I did not know where I touched
if my hand went nearly through. Like that.

And how was I to have known, that day
I brought you to the amphitheatre, which of the elements
    conspired, and to have removed even one—
the traveling hyacinth, or the memory of torchbugs
    in the mown grass—would suddenly erase
the small, chalk-colored road being drawn.

Elegy in Which I Am Awake

I thought it would be another door
      opened in the body,
opened on a street
      where there is music, and
a little rain or snow falling,
      the sound of someone shouting
in the rain,
      and the new warmth
of bare feet in streetlight,
      blue field at dusk
and you are always
      stepping on bees. When you mentioned
there was thunder
      a car swerved, went over
the railing
      into a previous summer,
though the horn
      wouldn't stop for hours,
and steam rose
      from the hood like a horse.
No bodies were found. I like
      to think they boarded a train
in the breath length between
      windshield and dawn,
caught the rail in time
      for the whistle which expands
to a sky, and turned their backs
      on the cicadas. Now
the train wades into a field
      somewhere, out
beyond the moon's reflection
      in the center of the lake,
aisle lights flickering.
      Now it travels the earth.

II

New Year on Pleasure Island

What I did not know to make made itself
in vestigial hours between two o'clock

and dawn, when the shapes of birds
stitch together in my mind, and a single

cicada peels the air. Each letter I write
returns to water. I start one now and already

the flashy ceiling of a sentence
begins to fade, and I am left with nothing

but the island and its circuitous thought
like the bulb shards of sunsets in the reeds.

Without going to the place I had to go.
Without any of the particular things

I was told that I needed to make my life,
I walk again down this desolate bank, sitting

with the occasionally given happiness
of a cup with the last opaque drops

fingered, as the wet sand is fingered
by a blue roving thumb. There is no set time

for the clouds to lose their inherited gold,
no moment when the wind will stop

and the stenciled islands far out
melt into an even line. The last of

the season inserts its sun-wide button
into the waiting hole. The year is closed.

The Island

Beneath Hag's Head the water rises
    in whitecaps against streaks
of bird shit and shrimpy mud
    as the island floats into view
and is gone. For three days
    bad weather. Then one morning
rainbows off the cliff edge
    like a trick of metallurgy. Wind
peels bees off the heather,
    squeezes the yew to its whitest sap:
if I told you that I saw it
    out beyond the ninth wave,
forked and sloping as the fluke
    of a minke whale and unmoving,
like an inch of green lichen
    on gray-blue slate, would you say
I was weak to stay on land?
    The mist closes as a staggered
line of puffins needles a pure
    white tunnel through the fog,
and three hundred feet below
    the waves gather their dead
into a wall, with frescoes of ice.

The Crystal Cave

It was something else entirely. The cave
and its vastness, sure, and the old man
walking the fishing paths to the ground.
But it wasn't made of crystal. More like
the gaunt peaks of the Burren: all cavern,
with its lists of lichen and pocked rock.
I picture his beard, twig-burdened, full
of gray patches, the pale torchlight
turning veins on his skin to fish scale:
Merlyn walking over bones of puffins,
bones of sea albatross, speaking a door
in no language into the limestone wall.

Stratis the Sailor at Eleusis

after Seferis

Who will follow him to Hell,
along the empty bank with its mirrors made of stone
and the sound of water dripping in a distant land.
The hole in the grass is full of stars
after two thousand years, even the birds
point their songs west and east, always away
from the Levant. *Here a braid*
in the ground where the wheel spat up,
here a sprig of rue berries
carrying the dark residue of her lips—
No one says how the earth opened,
if it was quietly or loud, or like
the sound of a three hundred-year-old tree
snapping at the roots, or how the moon felt
shining on the rape. Still,
the door and the wound are holy,
the old men say, with the bones of thrushes
curled in satchels around their throats
to absorb the Evil Eye.

Persephone

Again she goes aground, seeking love
in the mouths of the little fish

nibbling the vein-blue toes
of the shipwrecked. *Death being male*

marries the body. Her white hand
dripping on the oar as the ferryman,

whistling Dixie, remarks, but hasn't she
come here before? Enough times perhaps

to memorize the iridescent sky
of the underground,

or how the last breath repeats
into the back of the throat, moth-winged,

or the pivot the blood makes
to interfere with the act,

as if his memory were a thing,
like a spearhead, the body

could dislodge. Now she sees it
appear on the water: the tower

made of ash and teeth: the crowning
minarets positioned above

stately double doors, and the nearly
perceptible stillness beneath.

Yet having these,
the decomposing wealth of the aeons

he summons her
from the gaze of heaven,

tasked with the impossible:
to be a wife

in the place where nothing lives.
Death being male

marries the body, but only
to mine is he faithful. For the first

thousand years she watches his breathing
in the night and feels something,

not love, a sort of grief
that hardens into a body

and becomes hers, sneaking out
to the libraries in order to learn

the language of the earthworms,
to become, if nothing else

less a tourist. But all they said was
My Lady, not *My Lady, when did you realize*

that you would never be free?
For five thousand years she wore

his body so well that she saw it
in all things: stars, moon,

their reflection on the iridescent sky,
and pretended that the beauty

of her sorrow was enough. Now
she enters the widening hall

of her home, descending the stairs
past the multiple colored layers

with her just-pubescent feet
vanishing on the marble

as far above the ocean
a gate of winds opens, hinges

smooth as the first winter,
and I toss awake

to a chill in the bedsheets
and the howling of some distant dog.

Lord's Prayer

Lord, rescue me from the desire to be loved
by you, or any other earthless,
cumulus, *yacht among the clouds*
god of heaven and going up.
I have a god and he tells me
we all go out, and even better
we go to fungus and live in tunnels
underground, with pipsissewa
and his nets of sweaty bells.
How could you account for our
small happiness amid the chandeliers
with all that caviar on your chin?
Her body with the doors flung open.
Lying down next to her and sin.
I perform the calculations of gentleness
and she gives in, O, every time.

Blodeuwedd in the Garden

Foxglove. Foot of cowslip. Slender

nettle. Her ankles crackling over

the moss like tiny bells. That she is, or at least

might be a woman made of flowers enters

the humbox of the bee. I coveted each

of her bodies in the long grass, the way

a single thought from her would nudge

a tulip in the crowded stamens. The tree

for example, with its scarified circles—

permanent, unfathomable—she counts

her age in lovers, the pink and russet

of her affections stained gradually, like

the warmth of hands after they have left.

Now she dances beneath the moon's

garden, with the glinting of the petals

like flecks of spittle from another severed head.

Phthisis: A Letter

Kind of you to show me your hand
after the lung had been coughed up.

Over a period of thirty-one days,
the tissues and veins swollen with

crystallized oxygen, your white palm
holding so many warm rose petals.

How I would sit and, during those
long hours, listen to your small voice

grown monstrous in the chamber,
like a half-breath navigating

the interior of an instrument, passing
the valved and hammered walls

that made it huge. And when you spoke
I would pretend not to notice

the papery red darting out and back in
from your lips, like a second tongue.

You, alive without the words. You,
who carried them until now. What

will they do with you in Hades
when you have to breathe the air,

and so obligingly respond with a rasp
of your remaining half-lung,

like the sound of a hand digging
in a pocket, producing nothing.

The Temple

I have wanted a body that,
like a cathedral bell,
could survive several years

with one glowing note
still resounding beneath
the skin. I have wanted

a body that, like kudzu,
would not stop growing.
The old men at the coffee-

house, nursing tin thermoses
with wrists now brittle and
dry: they should be great trees,

warrior-colored oaks gaunt
as ancient samurai, their hard-
earned muscle still frightening.

The morning I hiked
from Tenant Mountain to stand
barefoot on Shining Rock, I felt

naked. The quartz humming
like a chapel full of whispers:
I could have come from

any century. The memory
of Crete, sitting in the cave
where Cybele taught Heracles

how to hold a woman's heart—
slowly, like the song
of a white crane—

I wanted a body that could sit
like a growth of quartz,
sacrificing nerves

for a skin that echoes,
patiently waiting on
nothing in particular.

I wanted a body that,
like Valmiki's, could sit
nine years in the Himalayas,

ants building their mound
to the crest of his bald
head, watching thoughts form

slow as seasons, the
mountain sweetening his
insides like a blood

orange until, at last,
fully ripened by stillness,
the earth eats him.

After a Suicide

Taking with you some memory of the crabapples.
Of London and the cemetery fog. You
in a corner of the room, looking out
the bay window with all the nearly-
blue light on your face. Did you hear it
when it came, the breath most precious
for being last? Before it pressed
slowly out and through the groove
of the keyhole. Out onto the lawn,
like a hand of flute music stirring
the carcass of a bee. Is it so terrible
finally? Or as they say: all pomegranates
and ferrymen, the strict bloodless moon
each day on the underground lake,
afterlife in the darkness of tubers.
Are you cracking jokes now
on your sad long way to Mt. Katahdin?
But perhaps you are born already,
a gloved hand pulling you out
fresh and sinewed as a newly bit
nectarine, your pink butt smacked
hard as all the air and death bends
into a child. What is there left to do now
but thank you. Thank you for ever
giving me to you. Thank you for dying on time.

Ephesus

And not a few of them that practiced magical arts brought their
books together and burned them in the sight of all; and they counted
the price of them, and found it fifty thousand pieces of silver.
—Acts 19:19

The price of oranges had gone up
so I bought a pitcher of turnips.

I arranged them for days at the foot of the statue.

By the time I was done they were rotten,
with bugs crawling on the paper.

I powdered the shells of the oyster with my feet.

I belched the bell gong and sat with the ants.
It appeared appropriate to leave some blood,

so I cut a beet when no one was looking.

Later, a cardinal flew in from the hole.
She landed on a breast and asked, *Which statement is truer?*

I was lost.
I was lost, and then I was lost.
I could not sleep for not having found.
The thing I hadn't found was you.

By now I am an old man, but death is no nearer.

When I see him coming, he crosses
to the other side of the street.

I invite him to my soirées and he replies,

honeymooning in Palm Springs.
I believe him, because of the retirees in Palm Springs.

Alone, I carry my pitcher of turnips again.

I knock three times before entering.

The priests have come and pounded off her breasts with iron crucifixes.

I feel for a nipple in the dirt.

The Hermit, Having a Lantern

That it shone its octagonal window
on the rock was all but expected.
The mountain and its runnels. The moon
as it careened widely over him, its crystalline
loudness hurried by otters. I could see
where the road became cliffs and air,
the guardrail removed long ago
by the Tuatha Dé Danann. The sieve
of clouds uniformly blue. I wanted
patiently from the folds of his robe,
blue-gray against the chasm of rock
but not alone, thanks partially to Messrs.
Will Rider and Arthur Edward Waite,
who kindly thought to ink a small dog
chewing at the ankle. And myself,
unvisited as yet by the planets over Uranus
and the cartwheel of his sickle through the wheat,
swallow it whole, the lantern and the dog.

III

Salt

Do you remember the rain on the windows in that particular street

in Provence? Is that motor and deluge any different

than it was then? The stars and the warmness under them

where I sat with my feet on the porous rock, carving

a flute from the tibia of an elk, giving up halfway in,

calling it a dart blower for the children. What children?

Every once in a while I take it down from the wall

and shoot my big toe. Such delight, each time.

Flamenco

His brown hand over the guitar. A brown leather hand
opening and closing. *It is called flamenco.* I know Flamenco,

having met him in a cave outside Granada. Flamenco has no running
    water.
He starts his laptop with a generator. Like Ginsberg, Flamenco receives

on average fifteen letters a day. He reads them all.
To write a letter to Flamenco, you must find a cactus with a dead bird

on it. You must burn the cactus and eat the bird so that later, lying
face up on the dune, in the company of rattlesnakes and sylphs,

you will not get hungry and scare off your desire.
Flamenco does not believe in housekeeping. Flamenco

will let you wash the dirt off your own feet with water and lemon.
If you ask to see the daughters, Flamenco will pull out his collection of
    poisonous beetles.

Flamenco will not give you things to say to the mailman.
You must think of your own things to say to the mailman.

If you are old, Flamenco will help you cross the road,
but you will not know what road or which country.

Flamenco can show you how to find self-portraits of famous
    photographers
beneath the stacks of girly mags in the outdoor market of Guadalajara.

When you die, Flamenco will be there to ferry you across the big water,
but only if you bring him a bag of HoHos.

According to Flamenco, there are two ways of putting Tabasco
on your patatas bravas: not at all, and not at all.

At night it is possible to see Flamenco from outer space,
but only if he is wearing his green sombrero.

When Flamenco is wearing his green sombrero, it is best
not to see Flamenco at all, but instead to close your eyes

and keep thinking of Flamenco as you remember him: old, tired, dead,
   young, vigorous,
and almost certainly not wearing a green sombrero.

Strange Abundance

Who ate
the pomegranate seeds
you plucked
        from the rind, and left
in a bowl beneath
the hazel tree? Did
        the owl,
or only the shadow
of the owl? Or perhaps
        the moonstripe
of a mink vanishing
with its mouth full,
        and the question mark
of its tail gone
in foliage. Yesterday,
        a loaf of bread
with no shadow
gummed,
        so gently
it might have been
the rain. Now
        a non-rabbit
takes from the yard
at night, cuttings
        of a strange abundance
beside the picked
chickweed, and thick
        magenta-like
wandering Jew.
How did I know
        it wasn't you?
After the rain,
armloads of empty squash
        and cumquats.
Leave the cup

of black rice
        on the road, for
the procession
which comes at night,
        which does not wake you
but wakes
the mirrors of the house
        with a burning
yellow light. I wanted
you to know
        I picked
all the leaves off your kale
in the garden.
        You might have thought
it was the cat, but it
was me. I did it
        with my hands, then
washed my hands
in the blue shadow
        of the hazel tree.

Spell to Divert a Summer

For a year of silence I paid
with a tooth
planted in the garden. By April

it began to sprout. Before
we knew it, the day grew
inward, tuberous—

even our shadows learned
to be silent, shed
their skins on the shadows of others

like black pollen.
What grows in me
spreads to you until neither

knows its name. Like
a small winged thing
cocooned inside the heart,

or a frozen trilobite
curled like an ear. Only
the silverware seems to notice

the temperature changing
in our hands. Each day
the salt less, less

the water. Now the wine
like its vinegar ghost.
The songs I used to sing

drip from my mouth
like beads of oil
hardening to stones. One

good train and I know the wall
will cave in. Who
remembers the sound

your hand made once
against my hand.
Your shadow my shadow.

Alexandria Duet

> *Beyond the canal there still remains a small part of the city.*
> *Then follows the suburb Necropolis, in which are numerous*
> *gardens, burial-places, and buildings for carrying on the process*
> *of embalming the dead.*
> —Strabo, Geographia XVII 1

I. Antony

To him the city casts human shadows,
the walls a mosaic of arms and legs
in circular motions, a plaster orgy
with each suffocating pleasure laid
stone by stone. It breathes: city
and shadow, like a winepress
of bodies beneath the circling levant—

> what use Empire
> to the body's known world?

The streets folded, dropped
into the sea like black coins
over a balcony as a prostitute
singing to herself in the street below
lifts her voice to reach across
to the land of the dead, out beyond
the memory of torchfires over the water—

> and for one long moment he forgets
> the noise of Caesar's road
> pounding the harbor wall,

looks across the room
at his reflection in the glass—

lips half-curled: the face of a man
after eating the first lotus,
and falls asleep with his body floating over
the colored banners, over the windows
breathing into each other's mouth—

and the perfume of each door was half skin.

Away, the Damascus bell breaks
in the city's throat, hard as a lemon,
as each boat's reflection on the air
turns and departs for the other sea.

Ɵ   Ɵ   Ɵ

The god abandoned Antony twice.
First in the mild perfume of ankle shells,
the fuck-warmed tambourines
spun in the air like silver bowls

sifting hairs of wheat.
                         And a second time
slower, like the bulge of his face
on each mercury-colored denar
passed over stalls of amber and brocade,
dropped with the sound of running water

on a boat's tilting floor:
                         each thousand-
handed minute palming his features
to oblivion. Like that the god spent

and spent,
and never returned.

Meanwhile Antony
                 in bed, dreams of water
slipping over a river stone,
fingering smooth each porous line
like a tiny thread of bone
until the rock begins to move.

2. Cavafy

In his alcove the Alexandrian
slim, mustached, pours
chalk from a silk bag into a glass,
watches the light-dissolving flare

of the city's granules like mullein dust
in the glass bottom of his mind.
In it one person crosses a screen, meets
another like blue-fibered ghosts

in pipesmoke. One speaks: you can see
the mouth moving, and the other
grows imperceptibly heavier,
like a palm frond in no air. They gesture

and slow, then one forgets (the other
forgotten) and new figures swirl
onto the screen of his mind
as the city goes on rehearsing.

Θ   Θ   Θ

In the darkness of apples.
In the rooms with walls of ochre daylight

where the last drop in the left-out cups
hardens to shadow,

and the white dress hung on the line
is used to wrap day-old meat.

What he has left to say is windows,
bottles, a bulb going on

or out: the spare ingredients
of the city

dissolved,
worn thought-thin, mindful

of the slow progress of bird shadows,
the folded echo of a dropped dime.

And the occasional tremble
(attributed to a train

or car, which barely dips
its finger in your tea)

flutters the back wall of the pantry
like a saucer turned into a moth

and is felt by other cities:
the seismic palpitations

of the dead scraping their heels
on the river's glass. From one

dead city to another. From one
live city comparing dead,

whose each green-tinged elevator wire
circles with dead like dust.

Now he drinks from the river
that runs through both cities

(the living and the dead) falling off the edge
of one in brownish strings.

Falling down through time or up,
catching on the air

that dresses each water
where he drinks the city from his hands.

Ars Poetica

the Poet working with the knife
in his third hand . . .
—Odysseas Elytis

I pull the hand out of my pocket,
the vanishing hand.
I am glad that it is only air.
Soon I will be able to see through it
to your face
when I hold it over my face.
The keys I was using
will fall and land with a bright noise
in the emptying hall: lucky hand,
never again having to unlock
anything. Unable to carry
the visible
without dropping.
Pulling no weeds with the taste of wet dirt.
Now it will gather what it learned in sleep
to gather: the transparent.
That which grows inside
the chamberous shadow of the seen,
like the strings of birds, or
the indentions your pain makes
on the air. Faulty hand,
I will try to tie a knot
of invisible herbs
and fail, until it learns
how to build, how to take down.

Ellipsoidal

A second light source turns on
somewhere in the room, perhaps
in the small of your neck

and the flickering black curls
reflecting other lights: sundown
like burning resins, like feathers

lit on the outer hairs. It wasn't
him, or another him, or behind
the bright vault of our conversation,

but like a window opened
in the bottom of your glass, lit
and lighting, a hidden room, a hidden star.

Rabbit the First

Rabbit a shadow
read by the nose.
Rabbit afraid of the moon.

Rabbit with a hand of wind
on his back.
Rabbit sniffing the end of dusk.

Rabbit like a blue flame
in a paused field.
Rabbit blown out.

The Longing Room

Although there are roads for the light
which arrives at your window at dusk, a stranger
raising a leaf with a delicate hand
so that you may be seen by no one

but me, the branch, yourself,
the cat, the teacups, and not be anyone's—
like bells growing in the roots of the mountain
or flowers opening under the lake—

heard by no one, although from time to time
your name brightens in someone's mind
and your face on loan goes out
to flicker at the end of a hallway

like through a keyhole, your wrist or neck
disappearing from the room as I watch
the remembering, and your visited body
vanish in sections, as though pulled by strings

into a neighboring world. At night
you return to my bed like a ghost
smelling of otherness, and the name
stays in your mouth like a tooth

dissolving as you sleep. At times
I would forget, and I would go about
my life: sitting on a bench, or sifting
on the curb in and out of conversations

like long pink clouds of exhaust. But always
at noon I return to the room in time
to see your body re-puzzle from scattered
tufts and pixels of flesh, softening

into the torso with its familiar part-terrarium,
part-animal lurch of shadow and drift
of hair on the face, shoulder, and tilted
by strands of light. We went on like this

how long? Now it seems like the dream
of being locked inside the same closet
for thirty years, only after we've woken up
we're thirty years older and unable to account

for the vanished center of our life. This
new silence made a road, in autumn,
in spring, through a field which went on
with only this scrap of gravel

to touch or be touched on, hiding
my hand in a wall of yellow wheat,
with the ghost of a wheelbarrow turning
a stone-gray wheel in a rut. I cut

my mouth on something I had begun
to say—tripping, and lost your hand
beside me, where the wheat is,
where the wheat goes on for miles.

Ode to Future Thirst

Each night in darkness
a man on the roof beats
a red nude
out of his violin

& each night
a village rises
to the roof
of my mouth: hot. I pluck

it out cicada by cicada.
His shadow hisses
touching water.
His face is

the face of a goat. I know it.
Carry the lantern
until the flame
grows too heavy. Wear

the furnace's
stagnant blood. If
you drink
from the bowl left out

you may lose
all your memories,
but only the ones
of this earth.

Gion

Somewhere where you cannot see them
the dead are making paper bells

and stringing them together, one to the other, via
the last remaining branches in the city,

without touching the birds
or the tiny squares of light

from off the paper windows. At times it seems
when you walk past at dawn

threading your new shadow out in front,
and the old one folding

carefully behind, a word of static
enters the street—touching

the filaments of the ginkgoes,
and the smoke-thin bones

in the palms of the leaves. But if
you were to call up to them

or to hold your breath
the time it took to count

to sixteen, they would close
their hands at once, and reach instead

to touch your hair, as if to figure out
which one of you

had happened before. All
that time, their delicate fingers

vanishing in and out of the world,
pressing a seam before folding

the new corners and distances of your life
like white paper.

The Road

after Cavafy

The latest on the road from nowhere is your going
and coming out the end of it, somewhere near Ithaka.
Cavafy said, do not seek riches in Ithaka, for once
you get there, Ithaka will only be Ithaka, and you
will be the one who went on the road to Ithaka,
who survived his own desire for Ithaka, and found himself
at the other end of desire, still alive, somehow,
and capable of making the little fog breaths.
I wanted Ithaka and its Cyclops, on the road. I wanted,
somehow, to be defeated by the road. Instead I am the road
defeating the Cyclops and Ithaka, defeating
desire itself. Alone with this wanting nothing but the road.

Previous titles in the Carnegie Mellon Poetry Series

2015

The Octopus Game, Nicky Beer
The Voices, Michael Dennis Browne
Domestic Garden, John Hoppenthaler
We Mammals in Hospitable Times, Jynne Dilling Martin
And His Orchestra, Benjamin Paloff
Know Thyself, Joyce Peseroff
cadabra, Dan Rosenberg
The Long Haul, Vern Rutsala
Bartram's Garden, Eleanor Stanford

2016

Something Sinister, Hayan Charara
The Spokes of Venus, Rebecca Morgan Frank
Adult Swim, Heather Hartley
Swastika into Lotus, Richard Katrovas
The Nomenclature of Small Things, Lynn Pedersen
Hundred-Year Wave, Rachel Richardson
Where Are We in This Story, Sarah Rosenblatt
Inside Job, John Skoyles
Suddenly It's Evening: Selected Poems, John Skoyles

2017

Disappeared, Jasmine V. Bailey
Custody of the Eyes, Kimberly Burwick
Dream of the Gone-From City, Barbara Edelman
Sometimes We're All Living in a Foreign Country, Rebecca Morgan Frank
Rowing with Wings, James Harms
Windthrow, K. A. Hays
We Were Once Here, Michael McFee
Kingdom, Joseph Millar
The Histories, Jason Whitmarsh

2018

World Without Finishing, Peter Cooley
The End of Spectacle, Virginia Konchan
Big Windows, Lauren Moseley
Immortal Village, Kathryn Rhett
Last City, Brian Sneeden
Black Sea, David Yezzi